DIANE WAKOSKI

DANCING ON THE GRAVE OF A SON OF A BITCH 🌼🌼🌼

Black Sparrow Press - Los Angeles - 1973

LIBRARY OF CONGRESS CATALOGING IN PUBLICATION DATA

Wakoski, Diane.
   Dancing on the grave of a son of a bitch.

   Poems.
   I. Title.
PS3573.A42D3   811'.5'4   73-16395
ISBN 0-87685-180-4
ISBN 0-87685-179-0 (pbk.)

Some of these poems have appeared in the following magazines: *Antioch Review, Bones, Bricoleur, Denver Quarterly, Odda Tala* and *Poetry Bag*. Acknowledgement is also due Walter and Mary Hamady of Perishable Press who first published "The Purple Finch Song" and "The Owl & The Snake" as broadsides, and to William Young of Sans Souci Press who first published "The Diamond Merchant" in a limited edition.

Thanks and appreciation to the John Guggenheim Foundation for a grant on which some of the poems for this volume were completed.

TABLE OF CONTENTS

THE ASTRONOMER POEMS

DANCING ON THE GRAVE OF A SON OF A BITCH

SOME POEMS FOR THE BUDDHA'S BIRTHDAY

THE DIAMOND MERCHANT

ESOTERIC FABLES

for the King of Spain whose footprints
I find wherever I go—

THE ASTRONOMER POEMS

SOME BRILLIANT SKY

David was my brother
and killed himself
by the sea,
a dark night
without city lights
to obscure the milky way.

My hair glistens around me like stars
on the night when a man
cracks in half and falls
into the ocean.
Sheets of water,
as I come out of sleep,
no lover,
only the sweaty body of dreams

                                 he stands over my bed
                                 as I wake up
                                 silent,
                                 whispering to himself,
                                 "no scars,
                                   no scars,"

but he forgets
David who died in the ocean
when the stars were visible in some brilliant sky,
and does not see my belly
mangled with scars
from childhood or birth.

Poetry is our history.
We study the stars
to understand temperatures.
Life and death are the only issues;
we often forget that—
arranging our furniture,
washing our cars.

When I look at the sky
I think of David
throwing himself off that cliff
into an ocean which moves with the moon,
dying,
the red blood in his mouth
in a night as black
as eels.

IN THIS GALAXY,

I looked for
a man who knew the temperatures
of stars; one
who
could draw rings around Saturn with a fine pen
and would sleep with me
as if a shower of meteors was a common occurrence
around the bed each night.

But love
and science—they are both gambles;
and if you try to win
the sun's light,
            you must be prepared also
to lose every
            day.

A FEATHER IN YOUR CAP

The pansies were too purple this morning.
Your face bit at mine
            like an hysterical doberman bitch.
The lawns were too green;
nothing in nature was past tense
                        present indicative
                        future imperative.
The sun,
your sun,
burned past my throat.

Who are you?
Not someone I know?
Not my King of Spain,
not my fiery sun god,
not the death of the novel?

You were a reminder
of how alone I am,
how beautiful and heavy with pain the world is;
what could I be?
but a feather in your cap?
this small bird that I am—finch or sparrow—

My pain
which makes me sing.

The pansies were too purple
this morning
too beautiful.
They arrested me in flight.

I invented a new tense:
            the repeating past/
all history
is natural/ all knowledge
accompanied
by pain.

THE MOON IS ONLY AGGRESSIVE WHEN YOU ARE THERE

                    pale,
                        receding,
                            the moon,
                                is only aggressive
when you are there.
On her surface.
Where you cannot breathe,
where her atmosphere has no meaning,
but aggressively assaults you
because it is not yours.
                    And the sun,
old fire ball,
too hot for humans
to be within a million miles of,
does it care
that you would melt on its surface? Surely it is not
hot
just to hurt you?

And you,
your face,
your eyes that have often seemed like predatory wealth to me,
you do not mean
to be my enemy.
                    But sometimes
you are
another world,
one where I am choked and cannot breathe,
where blood must run out of my nostrils in pain
as the vessels burst in my head.
You do not mean to hurt me;
I can only say,
however,
that sometimes
            you
                do.

THE STARGAZER

I read
in the newspaper today
that a tiny wasp may rescue dying American elms,
the old war of babies,
the fastest growing larvae eating others up,
you learn to fight back,
to take what you want,
to eat a lot
and protect your sleep
when you're young;
                    I look at the stars
on this clear night
with corny thoughts about distance and time,
wondering what it means
to survive,
if you have to eat others
to do it.

AN ODE TO MY FAVORITE ASTRONOMER

since you are the only one
I know . . .

but then
how could a girl in love with the sun,
who fancies herself to be the moon,
how could she not
fall in love with the natural historian,
the one who defines her life?

This is a rhetorical question
                        like,
will the sun rise tomorrow?
or
is the snow cold?
or
do you remember
my name?

IN THE SECRET ROOM, EAST OF THE SUN, WEST OF THE MOON

I met a magician
there,
measuring waves of light,
reflecting mirrors against my wrist
and touching me in the dark
of my own night.
I asked him for formulas,
remedies for my invisibility,
offered to trade him
the cap of darkness
for the magic ring
which would lead me through a garden
where flowers had daggers concealed in their petals,
the birds were flaming objects hurled against
intruders in the night,
and where a dragon named Love
guarded the gates against anyone
who had ever shed tears.
                              But he
would not trade,
saying,
it was not in his power.
And he sent me away to an island
where the sun only shone
one night of the year,
where there were no moons,
and the only light was phosphorescent, glowing
seaworms
which crawled up on the land
looking for something
nameless and beautiful
at a signal from a dragon named Truth.

But there were no magicians here,
or astronomers.

They were all somewhere else,
playing tennis with their glamorous friends.
I ate marigolds
and went home,
no longer afraid of anything.
But sad.
Feeling the loneliness
of my cold name.
I live in a secret place,
behind a carved door.
My house is a diamond and my life
is unspoken.
There is music that rescues us all,
and light into which
we all fade.
Life is its own metaphor. Silence speaks
for itself.

THE MIRROR OF A DAY CHIMING MARIGOLD

Astronomer,
I strike my gong for you.
It is gold.
Ancient.
Engraved with a calendar
of my heart.
And I strike it.
It rings
loud and melodious,
the sound of seashells,
the shouting of marigolds,
the angry book of dragonflies,
thunder,
an erupting volcano,
my heart pounding in exhaustion.

I strike it,
and it sounds for you.
As all of us are instruments
recording the heart,
playing its jealous and beautiful sounds,
the mirror breaking and shattering
past our tongues
when the fire burns our skins.

The astronomer looks at the sky and sees
all the phenomena of light.
This one gives himself a solar corona
while I stand in the shade of the moon.
                                          There is
an ancient priestess
whose tears make the spiderlilies grow.
She knows my name is darkness.
We are sisters.
As my tears are the blue lilies of the nile themselves,

my tongue,
a stamen waiting to be touched by the breath of insects
my life, a rock;
I look for a poet,
an astronomer,
one who studies
        my moon.

THE SUN HAS AN ANGRY FACE

and I dont want
to make him angrier/ today
                    I know
that he cannot
think of anything but his own
problems.
The fires that burn my wrists
when I am not careful
and want to ask him
to love me
are dangerous too.
And he,
scorching the grass
singeing the tops of tree,
burning the moon with her own stone tears
is angry.
I forget my sun
has an angry face
too.

MEETING AN ASTRONOMER ON
THE BUDDHA'S BIRTHDAY

Vanity
guards us
from introspection.

What guards us
from vanity?

To think of ourselves
like the moon,
dead and beautiful,
and of an origin no one
can be sure of?

I TAKE GREEN GREED ONTO THE FREEWAY

Speeding through the night,
the city spread out
          black
a garment
below me, the wide
          highway,
              empty,
as the night desert
wraps me
into myself. I am returning
from talking
to the King of Spain.
Returning into a night
with the fragrance of oranges,
returning with the night
whispering its silence
into my
ocean.
      I am alone
with the fabric of darkness
relieved by that solitary highway
studded with red lights,
the world below me full of the flashlights of life.
I am relieved at
the dark, the quiet, my own breathing, the silence
of my own poetry.
      Talk being cheap,
            the world being overpopulated,
I know what it feels like to be the tiger,
silently walking the night,
just wanting to live
his own life.

LOOKING FOR RABBIT TRACKS ON
THE FREEWAY

the
what-
way?
        The Free-
way.

What is freedom?

        When the rabbit can leave his tracks
        and you still cant find him,
        that's freedom.

And I remember a man
we all loved
who could walk in the woods
even in the city
tracking animals

but he was not free,
                was haunted
by the idea of the night,
haunted by too many voices, mostly
                        his own.
Moved to the woods
and there
never saw a rabbit.

I drive alone at night.
I tilt the rim of the world.
The lights are like raddishes in a bowl.
My foot is a cabbage/
lettuce flutters across my wrists.
The moon
leaves its light
behind

and the cars rake it up
like mulch to cover the night plants.

When I am with you,
                 I think . . .
                             Then remember,
that I never will be
again.

Freedom?
What is that?
When you are alone
                    and no one notices?
Another word
for
    the moon?

THOSE TRIGGER FISH AGAIN

Outside my window
the darkness
is complete.
For once,
I am not frightened by it.
I feel it swim past me
like some porpoise
I would touch with pleasure.

You are not
outside my window,
old man,
not part of that softness which is the new night.

When I see you,
you are a brilliant dying sun,
ready to gobble several planets from the solar system
before you flare out.

Knowing this vision of light
at last I can love the darkness;
at peace.
Away from the terrible fires
that once burned me up.
As if I was the smallest planet in a tight orbit.
As if I had no chance against
that space,
that night.

FIGHTING MY WAY UPSTREAM, A GAR, A BLUEFISH, IN MY FOOT

and the highways
were part of the night in my brain
and the black night spread
like glistening caviar
—the bread of my simple life—
the moon of my hands
the fish of my amazement
the owls flying out of the pockets of my wrists.

Every world I enter
is empty.
Until I get there with my trunks full of old letters,
valises with moon, stars,
an old ocean spilling out with silk dresses
and scarves
a foot locker of diamonds and discarded
mustaches.

At times
I am tired of life
and of the empty planets
the galaxies of silence
my only company, an occasional selenologist.

But our lives are simple
and all we have;
we drive the same highways
in the dark, not seeing each other,
                                        only the lights.
We fight our way upstream,
cold blood pulsing
until it is almost warm.
Fighting.
Moving.
To prove
WE ARE ALIVE.

WHEN BLACK IS A COLOR
BECAUSE IT FOLLOWS A GREY DAY

Could it all be
a question of contexts?
                    That I would not love
you
in some other world?
Or if you had another shape?
That to change wine into vinegar is a history
and that one state has nothing to do with another?

I drive along the rim
of the world.
It is night.
The lights below
are dew shaken off an orange at breakfast.
In this land,
dark comes as a color,
vivid,
burning,
a luster
after the grey of many days.

That I do not love anyone
in this night,
so brilliant I am trying to understand it:
that is a proposition
like the lumps of sugar that fall into
what they call
"a black cup of coffee."

THE GOLD FISH IN THE COOL NIGHT

It hangs
around someone's neck.
It glows
as something outside your
                          night
                               window,
perhaps a cigarette
on the porch out there,
summer holding air in its hand
until it is damp and heavy and warm
with the life of that hand,
its cigarette
on the porch
in the dark.

I am not asleep,
love that time of dreaming of the images
of strong men
with mustaches
who would love me,
who would find me in my bed at night, alone,
who would be starry and hot,
entering the dark room,
walking silently over to my bed, the cigarette
burning in a steady hand.

My own hands shake,
declare I never could have been a pianist,
never a painter,
never anyone who needed the hand to guide the heart or mind
into their beautiful forms.
My hands shake,
tho my heart
my brain,
my lips
         almost never do.

Night touches my wrists
it is my only steady lover,
coming regularly
more regularly than my own breath.
Ideas
in things.
   Yes,
      random and simple,
gesturing towards
the reality I believe in but have never known,
a man to love me faithfully
and passionately
who would locate me
when I am lost in my own ideas,
the ones that glow
hang around my wrists and neck,
like gold.
Gold fish in a cool night.

THE COOL STAR

She has it
in her bedroom,
corridors are dark at night
shooting stars
like blurred
images,
       faces in the rain
       seen through a window.

The past,
a tree:
       spruce,
       pine,
       cedar,
lighted for Christmas.
A pagan celebration.

FOR GARY, WHEN MY HANDS ARE OVER
THE SUN

And the sun walked in
dressed like
my uncle,
        a flamenco dancer in Spain.

He flashed his smile,
a rhythm in his boots,
a desperate journey in his hands
reminded me
of how warm your body is at night,
and how cold I am,
like a little stream of moon light coming in
through the raised window.
I could sleep with you forever;
I could lie beside you
and touch your body which is full of the sun
and make a whole world out of those nights.
But somehow
they would all criticize me,
with magnifying glasses capturing a beam of sun.
To light forest fires.
To illumine the hem of my dress.
They would all
heap snow on my doorstep
and freeze my fingers white.

When the sun walked in
like my uncle
I wanted to touch him,
as I want to touch you now,
my King of Spain,
the man I set my hair on fire
for.

I wanted to touch him.
But he was the sun.
He never wore a disguise.
You both rule my country
                          now.

Is it Spain?

SUN GODS HAVE SUN SPOTS

I dont care if you are
the sun god;
the flames leaping out of your eyes
flash,
turn green,
remind me that I might be looking at the god of rattlesnakes
those tongues of fire and light we see
dancing on the sun.

And if you are consumed by your own fire
And if you are a dying star
And if you are so active on the tennis courts
And if you have 12 girl friends
And if you are 6 feet tall
And if you are Russian
And if you drive a Mercedes
I dont care about any of those things.

Because I know this secret.
I am
also a ruler of the sun,
I am the woman
whose hair lights up a dark room,
whose words are matches
who is a lion
on fire,
      burning in the woods,
at night.
Women
they say
keep
the home-fires
burning.
      The first man to land
on the sun
will scorch his feet.

WHAT COLOR IS THE MUSTACHE OF THE SUN

Fiery red?

It has a corona?

It is so bright you cannot see it?

It is a golden cobra and never stops moving,
does not ever touch your
lip?

It is dark, turns itself away,
touches me,
in the night?

It is impulsive?

I am in love
with the sun?

WHEN YOU THROW AMBER INTO THE WELL OF THE MOON

A face looks out at me
from the water,
a lion shaking his mane and roaring
with anger at his watery trap.
And I reach my hand
into the water,
              like the slender trunk of a palm in the
              distance.
In the water
everything disappears.
Like a child in a crowd.
But the moon is death.
Its cold rocks fill my belly as if I had
swallowed songs of birds
and awakened in a tree.

When the sun died
it still lasted for thousands
of our years.
Magicians study it now,
while poets fly off to the moon.
My lion is trapped
in the water
which is desire.
And I throw my hand in
to rescue him.
But my hand cannot play tennis
or golf
or even the piano, anymore,
it is a useless hand
to a lion.

The crab sitting at the bottom of the well
looks up at the lion,
his eyes on stalks that are longer than my arms can reach.

He
is in his element.
Does not understand our struggles.
Music and poetry
only reach the ears
of those in anguish.
The silent crab
needs nothing
but the boom of the surf,
the pounding of waves,
even in the quiet well.

WOLF FIRE

It is
burning.
Your throat is on fire.
Your eyes light up with fire.
You run and the tail flames behind you, a plume, a burning
branch.
How can you steal fire?
When you are on fire?
The sun.
It is not your relative.
Or mine.
Except in the mind.
The mind
which is on fire.

I AM THE DAUGHTER OF THE SUN

shine,
it flushes my face
with marigolds.
My open hands brush against the raingod's face
and he steams,
boils.

Love is
not a visit to the bank.
Passion spends ahead of its
income.
Rain
here
is warm.
Night everywhere
is painful.
A sharp edge against the cheek.
A piece of broken glass under bare feet.
A mirror for scorpions.

When I am alone,
I feel like a day-old glass of water.
Night is bad poetry,
sentimental songs,
cold rain,
bad checks drawn on a non existent bang.

There is only one story:
that is the truth.
When it is too painful,
the narrative ends,
plot never was,
singing

or is it the rain?
starts.
The truth is my face.
I do not want to look in the mirror.

COUNTING SHOOTING STARS IN THE EYES OF AN
INVISIBLE OPPONENT

I woke up
in these woods,
and your face was the face of a fox.
The eyes shaped like a comet's orbit.
eliptical,
pointed nose and chin,
all staring down on me.

I thought you loved me
but knew Foxy-Loxy
from a story book
and thought for a moment in the
dark
as I sat up
and then looked down at your
winterwhite arm,
perhaps I was looking into the
wide-open jaws
of a cottonmouth.

But I loked back at your face.
You jumped
as if you had tripped on a fallen branch,
and the face
I memorized in the dark
was a face
I will carry with me,
one perhaps with a gold tooth,
the comet eyes—
my King of Spain,
someone I will remember
on a night
when I sleep alone

counting shooting stars.

TRYING TO READ BY THE LIGHT OF SHOOTING STARS

No wonder
my eyes are going bad,
this light
flashing—
more like a chalk mark on a blackboard
or the gleam on china
when you're eating expensive
food
and I cannot see
you
standing over there in the shadows,
can't see if you are with someone
or if another girl
has her arm
on your shoulder.
                    So tall
and the campfire gone out.
I thinking of someone lying so quiet
on the ground
that a snake might crawl over the ankle,
wondering why we read the words of poets and philosophers
while we look at the stars
wishing that we were astronomers.
Wondering why we have invented a world
that explains and reproduces shooting stars
without giving anyone
the satisfaction
of love.

MARKET SCENE ON A HALF MOON TRIP

My hair
is like the angels,
        they say,
                it shimmers
with something like
faith.

Gold and silver
moon and sun
some astronomer should love me
seeing my reflection
in his own ordered world.

But perhaps
there are many ways of viewing
the sky.

I ride all the way
to the temple of ancient beings
and find there
the calendar to my heart.

Open me up, I say,
to the ancient warriors
but they have served
fiercer hearts than mine and look
away.
My hair glints at them.
The knife recognizes
its kin.

All the light in the world
will not penetrate my darkness.

The dark room
locked
with iron
into my head.

THE DREAM OF ANGLING, THE DREAM OF COOL RAIN

I fished for the sun
but it was in a deeper lake;
I fished for the moon,
but it was my own face;
I found I could not swim,
but that water would be my house;
I found a boat called "Diane"
but it sailed past me
in every dream.

I was a neighbor of sharks,
till my arm bled at dawn,
but the man who loved me
sailed a big ship.
Blood was his cargo.
With blood he wrote my name.
That was a boat called "Diane."
Its name painted/ red paint on the hull.

I was a woman
in a man's world.
I was a fish
where there was no water.
When water flooded my life,
I could not swim.
One name is all you can have
in your lifetime.
It is a name
that will always be written in blood.

EXCHANGING A ZEBRA FOR YOUR FAVORITE
GIRL/DESERT/MOON

The dialogue is what is
important.
The moon tilted over in the sky
like the ring in my ear,
gold against my neck
                    in sleep
where all important activities take place.

Shyly,
        I look for
the taboo:
rhymes in stories
and fresh vegetables in Spain.

Kings knock on my door at night.
But I am solitary
like the owls I never see.

Flying through moonlight
their beaks curved against blood;
my eyes with holes in them to indicate
some servitude
to gold,
to the moon,
to the men who have held me in darker nights
than I can imagine.

Once more I hear
a conversation which never takes place;
while the rings burn their soft gold into
every night
and the owls I never see
hunt for some blood
which also
means nothing to me

except as an excuse
for my love,
           my dialogue.

A TIGER WALKS THE STREETS OF AN OLD TOWN

His name was broken in two.
His soft foot was also tough.
And I found gold scattered
in petals near
a fountain
that he passed
        on his way
to see me,
this beast of the jungle,
who lived only on the marigold balcony
of my imagination.

The map was a wishing well.
A garden of begonias
stood in his way.
The tiger belongs to another world.
I ride him in my dreams.
But my own eyes are fixed on the sky.
My map is the sun,
my tears are the moon,
Venus rises in my heart
        sometimes
at dawn
and sometimes
at dusk.

My life is a diamond
cut only
by a master
whose knife never slips
though it comes close to my throat each day.
When I rise
in the morning
it is over a well of clear water.
My shoulders slope down

like gardenias
and camellias.
Their fragrance
is the map of a poet.
He will cry when he sees the moon's reflection,
but his heart is too near the knife
for breath.
I have spoken twice
to an angel
but only once in a garden.
Once so near death
that I do not wish
               ever
to see angels
again.

FOR WHITMAN

I have observed the learned astronomer
telling me the mythology of the sun.
He touches me with solar coronas.
His hands are comets with eliptical orbits, the
excuses for discovering planet X.

Lake water shimmering in sunset light,
and I think of the whitewashed dome of discovery
hovering over the landscape
wondering what knowledge does for us
in this old and beautiful un-knowing world.
                                    Yes,
                                        I would

rather name things
than live with wonder
or religion.

What the astronomer does not understand about poetry
is the truth of disguise.
That there are many names for the same phenomenon.
Love being
the unnamed/
the unnameable.

DANCING ON THE GRAVE
OF A SON OF A BITCH

These poems are dedicated to Jerome Rothenberg who has reminded all of us of our poetic origins/ with appreciation for his magnificent Poland 1931.

INTRODUCTION

This winter was the first time it occurred to me to try to put a book of chanted poems together, though obviously these little poems are the result of one of my concerns in writing. To make the spoken word, the poem, into its own music.

I do not want to write words for music, but rather in all my poems, even the most talky and prosaic, to have the words create a kind of music themselves.

Needless to say, the poets who have taught me the most about this are Jerome Rothenberg, Armand Schwerner, Jackson Mac Low, and Paul Blackburn.

All of the poems in this set are meant to be read aloud in a special fashion. The first poem is an exception to this, as part of it is simply an ordinary poem, but it is interspersed with chanted parts. The first poem which I wrote, which I have always wanted to be read as a chant, was part of a series of poems using imagery from the tarot deck. It appears in my collection, *Inside the Blood Factory*. and is called "Sun." When I wrote it, I did not thoroughly realize how adamant I would become about wanting it to be read in a certain way. Now that I am aware of that, I write chants into my poems often, and do wish that the reader would be cognizant of those parts, and treat them specially when he reads them aloud.

I've tried to set the poems down on the page so that you could read them in the most rhythmical way possible and could even program some of them for several readers or antiphonal performance. I would also like to say that I believe the cognitive aspect to be the most important one to me in poetry and would not want this element of spoken music to take over, either in a majority of my poems or in a majority of the lines of any poem.

I have put this small collection together to point out this aspect in my work and to call attention to a kind of reading aloud in poetry which turns me on whenever I hear it. I think that Sonia Sanchez and Jerome Rothenberg are the best exponents of it that I currently know. They have much to teach us all.

This poem is more properly a "dance poem" than a song or chant because the element of repetition is created by movements of language rather than duplicating words and sounds. However, it is in the spirit of ritual recitation that I wrote it/ a performance to drive away bad spirits perhaps.

The story behind the poem is this: a man and woman who have been living together for some time separate. Part of the pain of separation involves possessions which they had shared. They both angrily believe they should have what they want. She asks for some possession and he denies her right to it. She replies that she gave him money for a possession which he has and therefore should have what she wants now. He replies that she has forgotten that for the number of years they lived together he never charged her rent and if he had she would now owe him $7,000.

She is appalled that he equates their history with a sum of money. She is even more furious to realize that this sum of money represents the entire rent on the apartment and implies that he should not have paid anything at all. She is furious. She kills him mentally. Once and for all she decides she is well rid of this man and that she shouldnt feel sad at their parting. She decides to prove to herself that she's glad he's gone from her life. With joy she will dance on all the bad memories of their life together.

DANCING ON THE GRAVE OF A SON OF A BITCH

for my motorcycle betrayer

God damn it,
at last I am going to dance on your grave,
old man;
      you've stepped on my shadow once too often,
you've been unfaithful to me with other women,
women so cheap and insipid it psychs me out to think I might
ever

be put
in the same category with them;
you've left me alone so often that I might as well have been
a homesteader in Alaska
these past years;
and you've left me, thrown me out of your life
often enough
that I might as well be a newspaper,
differently discarded each day.
Now you're gone for good
and I dont know why
but your leaving actually made me as miserable
as an earthworm with no
earth,
but now I've crawled out of the ground where you stomped me
and I gradually stand taller and taller each
day.
I have learned to sing new songs,
and as I sing,
I'm going to dance on your grave
because you are
      dead
      dead
      dead
under the earth with the rest of the shit,
I'm going to plant deadly nightshade
on your grassy mound
and make sure a hemlock tree starts growing there.
Henbane is too good for you,
but I'll let a bit grow there for good measure
because we want to dance,
we want to sing,
we want to throw this old man
to the wolves,
but they are too beautiful for him, singing in harmony
with each other.

So some white wolves and I
will sing on your grave, old man
and dance for the joy of your death.
"Is this an angry statement?"
                    "No, it is a statement of joy."
"Will the sun shine again?"
                    "Yes,
                      yes,
                      yes,"
                    because I'm going to dance dance dance
Duncan's measure, and Pindar's tune,
Lorca's cadence, and Creeley's hum,
Stevens' sirens and Williams' little Morris dance,
oh, the poets will call the tune,
and I will dance, dance, dance
on your grave, grave, grave,
because you're a sonofabitch, a sonofabitch,
and you tried to do me in,
but you cant cant cant.
You were a liar in a way that only I know:
                    You ride a broken motorcycle,
                    You speak a dead language
                    You are a bad plumber,
                    And you write with an inkless pen.
You were mean to me,
and I've survived,
God damn you,
at last I am going to dance on your grave,
old man,
I'm going to learn every traditional dance,
every measure,
and dance dance dance on your grave
                              one step

for every time
you done me wrong.

foreword to "The Purple Finch Song"

I am an amateur birdwatcher. Last winter I went to Wisconsin to visit some good friends who also enjoy the birds. While driving from the station they told me excitedly that they have Red Polls at their bird feeders this year. I think this is exciting because I have never seen Red Polls.

When we arrive at their farm and are sitting in the kitchen, a flock of birds land on the feeder. They are like sparrows only many of them are a deep magenta on the head and shoulders. They tell me these are the Red Polls. I say, "They look a lot like our Purple Finches out in East Hampton." Then I ask what the great numbers of little sparrow-like birds accompanying them are, but they do not know. After studying my Peterson guide for several days I come to the conclusion that the birds are indeed Purple Finches and not Red Polls, as those drab sparrow-like birds that always come with the colored ones are the female Purple Finch/ the males much darker than those in New York.

THE PURPLE FINCH SONG

for Walter & Mary Hamady

I.

We thought it was

       a
          Red-
              poll
                 RED-
                     poll
                         RED, RED, RED
                               poll

until we saw the
lady.

II.

When you
meet
the woman
you
come to terms
            with the species.

III.

Those handsome male purple finches
so royally bathed
in the juice of strawberries
had us fooled;
if you want the truth, you know,
you've got to meet
the lady.

A LITTLE MANTRA FOR BECKY'S BOX

silver fish
will twinkle over you
when you sleep at night.
a cover of feathers
from the snow goose
will slip under your sweet face,
and a hand that you love,
wearing a ring of jade
as if a piece of the ocean
had frozen, and rested on
a sliver of gold,
will touch
your cheek.
               in the night
that which is strong and
durable, hard and lasting,
becomes soft in texture,
as the most convincing touch
is gentle and cushioned.
love is an old story,
and always comes to those
who wait.

SNOW CHANT

snow bunting
                on my tongue
snow goose
                in my pillow
snow dog
                in my dreams
snow jade
                from the east
snow heart
                in my garden
snow apples
                filling the room with scent
snow trees
                that glitter with the ice queen
I've seen her
                the woman of snow
I've seen her
                in the thin branches of old trees
I've seen her
                in my own fingers
I've seen her
                on your lips
                which are 1000 miles
                away
I've seen her
                snow bunting
                snow goose
                snow dog
                snow jade
                snow heart
                snow apples
                snow branches
                snow woman
snow queen   ice queen
snow queen   ice queen

snow queen   ice queen
the silver of an old moon,
stuck in the corner
                of the eye

A SUNSET CHANT

```
glow                        sun
     oh                     sun
          there is          sun
                    a        sun
glow                        sun
     oh                     sun
          there is          sun
                    a        sun
                            sun
                            sun
                            sun
                            sun
sun shining on              sun
        the nape of my      sun
              neck          sun
                  I am          SET
                     filled          a
with winter sunset                        horse
my eye is a knife                              shaped
that cuts off the excess of day                    above
as if it were a thread                                  my hands
sticking out of a button
```

A CHANT FOR HYACINTHS

hyacinth
       grape
hyacinth
       willow
hyacinth
       bare branches
hyacinth
       lemon
hyacinth
       there are colours that wind
      around me
     like thin scarves
      like soapy water
      like the foam of the sea.

            Winter is a crystal.
            Spring is a pool.
            Summer is the way a ripe apricot
                         is nudged off a branch
            Autumn is a crackle
            a fire.
Now I Have Mastered The Four Seasons.
Should I Still Need Love?

hyacinth
softly glowing   A man's name
every March.   on my lips
Sometimes April.   thru all 4
                        of the seasons.

A CHANT FOR THE DWELLER IN THE DESERT SOLITAIRE

man
with a snake wrapped
around his waist
man
with a full coffee cup
in his hand
man
with a rifle
and a falcon on
his shoulder
man with a coyote
in his blood
cantankerous,
trickster,
wearing woman
like a deerskin moccasin
on the foot
you are   in my cardinal eye
      sparrow hawk
      sparrow hawk
      sparrow hawk
      sparrow hawk
I am
a kestrel
waiting
on a fence
post.

SNOWMAN CHANT

ice flakes
          sifting
          sifting
          sifting
on his head
on his head
               he is dead
               he is dead
oh,
snow,
        oh,
snow,
        oh,
snow,
        man.
               You are a cold son of a bitch
                    no sun
                         sun
                         sun
                         sun
                              in your face.
Shiver,
        snowman,
I have your sliver
of ice
in my eye.
          It burns.
          Why?
          It burns,
oh,
snowman,
oh,
snowman.
          You are definitely a cold sonofabitch

CHANT FOR A SHARP KNIFE

I am
I am
I am
I am
I am
I am
I am
I am
I am
I am
I am
I am
I am
       a sharp knife.
Dont lay
yr tongue against me.
Dont let
me rest w/out
a sheath
against yr thigh
dont let
me ring
like church bells
in yr kitchen
because
I sing
I sing
I sing
I sing
I sing
I sing

I sing
    of the steel
    you have never had the hot temperature
    to forge.
    You are the axe
    I have
    to grind.

APPLE CHANT, 1

pip
pip
pip
pip
pip
pip
    white flesh
    white flesh
    white flesh.

It is no
watermelon.

APPLE CHANT, 2

fire-crowned
linen-cheeked
an old anger
that turns into
love.

CHANTS/CHANCE

for La Monte & Marian

blue stone
      own
      own
      own   pock
      own   et
          one stone   pock
                      et
cracked rock   sock
whole wheat   it
blue death   sock
blue angel   it
blues   sock it to me
      cherry   blues
      cheery   blues
         eerie   blues/blues/blues
         eerie
         eerie
           the Erie (eer-i-e)
           Canal.

SOME POEMS
FOR THE BUDDHA'S BIRTHDAY

BUDDHA'S BIRTHDAY

A pile of lead
drippings
sparkling a mountain
made
from the shrine
of a
bird's eye
in the headlights. His beak
brighter.

Your anger
the way a bird is hidden
in the dark.

A LONG TRAINRIDE WITHOUT A CALENDAR SHOWING BUDDHA'S BIRTHDAY

A photograph of the Buddha
taken in 1936
reveals that he had
a mustache.

Calculating
all the faces
on this trainride
none could be
you.

In a compartment
maybe?
No amount of concentration
would produce
hair
on a bald head.

If this train were circling the earth
it would not join
parts
that give a man hair on his face
but none on his head.

LETTER TO CAROL BERGÉ
ON BUDDHA'S BIRTHDAY

I was
so agressive
that year
I would have written
a dozen books
published them
and sold them
from door to door
    like
    the
DISCRETE SERIES
if they had not removed my tonsils
and sewed the fingers of my gloves
together.

And fortunately
the world
received
your letter
warning everyone
not
ever
to let me in.

So
now
I want to wish you
happy zen year
and hit you over the head
o master
o pupil
o dot in my eye.

Three Buddhas were born
(at least)

one in Aries
one in Leo
one in Sagittarius.   It takes
fire to keep
the world
warm.

JUDGE NOT, SAYS THE BUDDHA ON
HIS BIRTHDAY

This rock?
            Elementary sediment.
Not valuable?
            It was valuable to the land
            it was part of.
It sparkles.
            So do your teeth. But they don't if
            you extract them.
            Nor will they be
            of any use.
Tisk, tisk, I
guess I'll throw all my diamonds away.
            Go ahead.
            Someone else will appreciate them.

THE BUDDHA LEARNS TO WORK A RADIAL
ARM SAW ON HIS BIRTHDAY

It's easier to burn
than to build.
Thousands of fireflies
put into a tank,
a bottle,
glow brightly
with enough light to light the whole garage,
cause no rise
in the temperature. They are the only
known
cold light.

This saw, I saw, with my own eyes.
Fireflies
glow in the dark
without burning;
I am learning that you can
build anything.
Is it true,
with all your power tools,
you make the
city run?
Do not confuse burning
with making light.
Or building,
with the tools that do it.

GEORGE WASHINGTON SENDS A PAIR OF
SHOEBUCKLES TO THE BUDDHA ON HIS BIRTHDAY

Sages
walk
barefoot
sometimes

thru history

as do patriots and soldiers
when they don't
have shoes.

But in case,
Dear Sir,
you are ever thinking
of appearing
formally,
a pair of shoe buckles
might be
in order.

My Lord,
I would give as much
to
any man.

A LITTLE POEM FOR THE CALLIGRAPHER
ON THE BUDDHA'S BIRTHDAY

Letters
you've chosen
to illuminate
catch me
when I ride
across country.
                    The Pony Express
carries
my letters
to you
          W
       X
         Y
           Z.
X,
of course,
is always
the unknown.   So,
shall we
look for it
in the sounds of the hooves
on the prairies,
listen for it
when silk
seems to move
at our feet?
                    When we find X
all the letters
will be in the same bag;
and of course
you will have drawn them
while dreaming,

will have plucked them out of your eyes
from your spicy fingers,
your inky
ears.

MY AUNT ELLA MEETS THE BUDDHA
ON HIS BIRTHDAY

She would like to roll down the aisles
of her church,
past the hard benches,
and in a frenzy
tell Sweet Jesus
she is holding his hand.
But though other members do,
Aunt Ella, in her soft
fried-egg body,
with two crooked fingers without nails
   (pushed into a machine in an aircraft factory during the war)
does not.

Her life,
        of course
cannot fit any testament.
Where did all the dirt come from
under the fingernails
when all she did
was try to lead a pure life.
       But a woman
       without a man
       is like a wild rose
       which blooms fast
       and flies away
       falls apart
       with the wind.
Her husband
killed in an accident
when she was like a new gardenia,
her skin white
the way girls do not like their skin to be today,
and her two daughters,
living despite her chocolate covered cherries
and true confession magazines

which warned
against all
that can happen in this world
where the innocent are butter
in a hot skillet.

      Helen,
            quiet,
                   with thick red lips and a pompadour
          married a sailor
          who ran off
          with his Australian mistress during the war.
I was a 10 year old kid
when Helen died.
The first dead person I ever knew/or saw.
The fact that none of us knew
how she died,
leads me to believe she killed herself,
the whispers were all there
but I wasn't old enough to piece them together.
Besides,
who ever tells children about death?
It is something we must learn about from
insinuation,
the innuendos of bitterness or regret
that make people say things
they don't want to.
Something must have happened
after that day her husband's plain plump mistress
came to the door and
said she was going to have a
baby
          this I heard whispered about
          in the pantry
          between my mother and Aunt Ella.

But they didn't whisper enough
after that
for me to hear
what happened to Helen
   or her thick lips
      that could have made her some Midwestern Protestant
      relation
        to Cleopatra.

Louise,
the other daughter,
married a truck driver,
6 feet tall,
who was often out of work,
who drank,
had other women,
spawned four children who all wet the bed
and had to come and live
with Aunt Ella.
Louise was a waitress
and she and her girl friend
died of carbon monoxide poisoning
sitting in front of the cafe where they worked,
in the old car,
having a cigarette on their break.

Aunt Ella lay alone at night
in the house with four grandchildren,
reading her true confession magazine,
praying and sure that those four
teen-agers were out doing
all the things
described in her magazine.
And I'm sure they were.
They lived a life that I,

scholarly, quiet, prissy,
could only be fascinated and put off by.

Aunt Ella had a friend, whom we called Uncle Noah.
He was a secondhand junk dealer,
a man who always wore a hat,
something uncommon in Southern California.
My mother told me he was very rich,
but he never spent his money.
He had been trying for years to get Aunt Ella
to marry him; but she was afraid
he might take her to bed
and try some of those things
described in the true confession magazine.
They went to church together,
but never rolled down the aisles;
though they must have shouted to God
many times;
and called on Sweet Jesus
to have compassion and some mercy
on their souls.

The title of this poem is a lie.
My aunt Ella never met the Buddha.
On his birthday, or any other time. The Buddha
scarcely ever goes where she does,
and she
doesn't like foreigners.
It is actually a common trait
in our family; none of us
really likes
foreigners.
Now isn't that down-home
American?

THAT DELICATE DISPLACEMENT OF REALITY
ON BUDDHA'S BIRTHDAY

A smile
is not necessarily filled with pearls.
Nor the orchid a sexual symbol.
Do you get the feeling
somebody's
putting you on
when people talk about what they believe?
Art is nothing
but that delicate
displacement—
George Washington with a mustache,
a poet with a gun,
a poem without any words.
How can people
base governments on what they believe
rather than what is practical
and useful?
Supply and demand
is not a street full of imitation pearls,
all rolling under cars and under
foot.
If they were real
it would not be more accurate
either. Who knows when
he'll find a pearl in his walnut
or anchoring a flower's root
to the earth?
Pay attention to
supply and demand.
It will prevent
wars.

BUDDHA HAS HIS BIRTHDAY IN COURT

You are accused
of
wearing
a black
beard
in a hairless country.

I deny the charge.

We have evidence:
witnesses,
photographs,
and a scrap of the thin
hair.

They are all lying.

Can you offer any proof of this?

No.

How can you expect us to
believe you?

I cannot.

Is this a poem?

*No, it is a manual
of a poet's
process.*

A CHAIN LETTER FOR LUCK ON THE BUDDHA'S BIRTHDAY

May fire flit its way
under your skin
like an opal under the tongue
of a swan.
Harsh
sounds
come from beauty.
They streak
through
smooth stone
marbling it,
        the shining stone
in the sky
is your wish
to be unlocked
from this chain
around
your neck.

Words glitter
around your neck,
infant,
swan imitator.
        May the suffering
we all do
pay for days
full of
poetry.

INSTRUCTIONS FOR GROWING LABURNUM
ON THE BUDDHA'S BIRTHDAY

black
& glittering
as a piece of licorice candy
after you've sucked it,
the poisonous seeds from this tree
fall
over the garden wall
careless
pods;
as the spots of light
change places,
glimmering here and there,
coming through the leaves and shining
on my yellow skirt

sitting in the shade
thinking
about the sun.

POEM FOR THE COMFORTABLE ON THE
BUDDHA'S BIRTHDAY

This flower
that drops
its petals
like the wrists of a Japanese
Lady's
poem,
floating
down the river
beyond anyone's concern,
gives me
an image
of a beautiful round white face,
jade at the throat;
can you make your poems outside of this courtyard,
where there is no fragrance,
where there are no soft quilts
or white feet?
Can you
replace
the stringed music
with the sound of war? No poet
writes from the city.
His words are the crickets
no one in the country
ever sees.

       Where are you
       writing
       from?

THE SCISSORS, A POEM FOR THE BUDDHA'S BIRTHDAY

The two parts
rely on
the tension
between them. A normal pattern
in natural
objects.
A cold day in spring
reminds me
of winter. My memory
relies on
pain.
My pleasure
on knowing I will see
you every
night.

THE BLUE WORLD HOLDS THE SUN AS A RAKE ON BUDDHA'S BIRTHDAY

A cold slice
on your
tongue
of peach or
melon. Perhaps of the knife
which you don't
feel
till the air hits the cut,
why you can bleed to death in the bath
and never feel it.
The world
makes shadows
as if there were hills
in everyone's
life,
bluish purple crests
that only exist
from a distant perspective.
Can you really
shape your own life
any more than a pregnant mother can decide
or determine what her child will look
like, though it's her body
that's the factory,
the designer?
Well, give me a handful
of whatever it is
that you use
for love. I'll investigate
the possibility
of sending
a letter
to my father;
he knifes the earth, saying he's plowing;

he burns my face and tells me
not to put so much faith
in the sun
or the ocean. It is you I think of
when I sit and look at the
shadows
in the hills
some evenings.

A MESSAGE TO SOMEONE I LOVE
ON THE BUDDHA'S BIRTHDAY

A tone row
   —a lot of notes lined up
      waiting to be knocked down
is not an argument
between
another concept
    (keys).

But
neither
does tone
mean
tune
   to get the right pitch
to find the key.

A tone
creates
an atmosphere. Say,
one of peace (piece?).

   I love you.

This is a note on
musicology.

POEM FOR A MAN WHO IS SLEEPING
ON THE BUDDHA'S BIRTHDAY

Strong face,
long mustaches,
thick legs,
I am confronted
with what we imagine:
an enchanted person, one under
a spell
      what goes on
      inside your head
      as you sleep
a waterfall
that has been lighted from beneath
could not be more spectacular
in this night.
Sleeping man,
I know
sometimes,
        whoever you are.

THE BUDDHA RUNS A RACE ON HIS BIRTHDAY

I wouldn't ever
write
these letters,
punctuating my pages with stories of insects:
         ladies in the West Indies
         walk to a ball
         wearing elater beetles
            iridescent,
              their asses glowing
         pinned into their hair,
         on their shoulders
         the insects lighting up the women,
         the glow worms
         making their shoulders flicker,
         their hair snap
         with concealed
         fire.
This is only the first page.
But I am racing to let my poems catch up with my mind;
birthdays come as fast
as the teakettle whistles. It is
not a fog horn,
or a train whistle.
Rushing into my fingers
or my mouth
is fire. Glowing
a sense of you
in the other room. Time passes
too quickly.

THE BUDDHA TURNS BASE METALS, FLOWERS & BUTTERFLIES INTO GOLD ON HIS BIRTHDAY

A little alchemy
cannot hurt
anyone.
Say, converting
a flower
into
a pair of gloves
or a Savage Tailed Blue Monarch
back into a piece
of silk.
But old tricks
teach us
to be wary.
The word
betrays
because it does not disclose
a whole process.

Love,
even,
is a betrayer;
taking my wet heart out
and planting it under the Buddha's foot in the garden.

THE BUDDHA MEETS SATURN

My thumbs
like two hammerhead
sharks
wage open war
with each other
over my typewriter.

This thumb is dry and cold
resides on the desert
at night.

My other thumb
chases rose bushes
into dark
wet
soil.

How do you do.

We say.

When we meet.

Two old gentlemen
both hail the same cab.

If we leave any finger prints
wherever we go
probably we will first
leave the thumb.

A little smile
is all we can afford for each other
when we meet
on the street.
My two thumbs
have not
even
a decent
hello
how do you do
a small smile, like a dried pear,
for each other.

BANK STATEMENT ON THE BUDDHA'S
BIRTHDAY

I count my money
after it's
already spent.

If I had a steady income
I'm sure I'd also have a
steady creditor,
someone dressed in a white suit in the summer
and a pencil in winter
to discreetly lift
the bills
from my hands,
from my impractical lace gloves
that even the coins drop through.

Once I thought
my investment
was
my brain,
my life,
my tongue & wit;
but look what happens to pensioners
with their fixed incomes . . .

My savings dwindle.

Dear Banker,
Kind Merchant,
watch the leaves
fall
from this
tree.

THE BUDDHA TAGS A FISH ON HIS
BIRTHDAY

Blue Pike,
fluting through
water,
not staying
for landmarks

the watermark
on this
paper
rubbed in
by hard water
that can touch the delicate skin
of dolphins
and not hurt it
as air
so soft to ours
might.

Come back.
Near this tree.
An oboe played in the forest.
Come back to my ten fingers
the smell of a star, burning Algol.
Come back through this map of currents
the lines on your face,
my friends,
when you smile,
when you think of the places beyond city,
the woods,
the water,
filled with Blue Pike.
                    The cup of tea
in which I see
some
reflection.

WILDFLOWERS FOR THE BUDDHA
ON HIS BIRTHDAY

Spring nasturtiums with small necks,
Lupin
      bells that ring when the comets fall.
Sweet William
Anastasia's Purse
Foxglove holding the
Lady's Slipper in this
Court of the Morning.

Blue Bells,
Hair Bells,
Belladona,
Thorn in the Waist,
Columbine,
Bleeding Heart,

I could not say
my love is
like
a
red red rose.

Wild rose.

POEM FOR A LITTLE BOY ON THE
BUDDHA'S BIRTHDAY

You have
taken
a complete biography
in the form
of your mother's hand. Such a camera
the lens
a blind measurer;
who cares
whether you will be president
if the coral scrapes
cuts the bottom of your feet as you walk
along the ocean floor,
who cares
where you are? Your mother never
forgets;
she does not however feel
the same salt.
        Is there anything
        more real
        than imagination?

She does not even
know where you are.

THE BUDDHA EMPTIES A VOLCANO ON
HIS BIRTHDAY

Throw out
all the stone
this is a form
of housecleaning
what will you do
with the mineral rights.

A ritual we all go through
rejecting the past
so that we can
relive it
in the present.
I would like to walk
along the edge
of a calm sea
and remember
water
covers
all future land masses.
Give me an atlas,
and I'll draw you some new continents.
One for each of your feet,
your hands,
a few to be reached by word of mouth.

THE ELEPHANT & THE BUTTERFLY MEET
ON THE BUDDHA'S BIRTHDAY

As the blue wings
brush by
the large grey dusty ear,
wrinkled and soft as a dried peach,
the butterfly
engages in
flickering reflection:
> no danger here.
> Because I couldn't be still long enough
> to be crushed.

The elephant
says he would like to visit her
in her own home.
This being too whimsical for the butterfly
she moves on.
A Camera.
A Secret.
A Way of looking at things.

I find certain subjects
sentimental;
the prison my face locks me in.

THE DIAMOND MERCHANT

THE DIAMOND MERCHANT

The son of the diamond merchant
comes out of the heap of stone shimmering
scintillating
glowing softly as a plum in the green leaves of summer,
the heavy foliage protecting
his color.

The son of the diamond merchant is born
knowing how to eat flesh,
thread it on a hook;
he takes diamonds out of his own mouth for his father
just as his father,
the alchemist,
took him
from the bag of diamonds in his body and
lifted him full of blood from some one else's body.

At an early age he confuses diamonds with the sound of rain
or the crackling of leaves in the night;
he confuses diamonds with his own breath
and the pulses in his throat and fingers.
The diamond merchant himself confuses the sunlight with the
flashing of his merchandise,
chases it in the afternoon
plays golf with it flashing in and out of the pockets in the ground.
The diamond merchant reads his newspaper
in the disguise of the astronomer,
fills his pipe with golf balls
and diamonds;
smokes a whole galaxy in his pipe.

The diamond merchant
created the diamond merchant's son,
confusing his mother
with the burnished dark grapes hanging in the summer arbor,

the round fruit not to be confused with the merchandise
in his pocket,
which he could never let go of.
The baby will not be a diamond
he kept telling himself,
but forgot there was anything else
in the world,
the sun periodically slipping into his mouth
and melting everything around
but the diamonds.

Dug out of the ground,
with no roots at all,
diamonds are the ugliest
most valued stones;
the diamond merchant who fondles them
keeps them in soft cloth bags,
becomes a purveyor of dreams with heavy jeweled fingers,
fleshy tubes lifting stones out of his pockets
that will buy a woman,
or a whole life.

Sometimes they are the sun,
burning in his wrists,
when he comes home at night
the diamond merchant
black hat and suit
and eyes that are worn at a woman's throat
the eye itself
which burns or which flickers in
its pronged setting.

The diamond merchant at work
is ready to grind and polish a life;
he looks for those spots,

the long roots of a tooth,
filled with blood
where he can focus and discover the expensive fiery axis.
He always asks the question,
"Who will pay for it?"
and
"How much?"

He examines every new star he finds cracking out of his
        precious stones,
every crystal,
every shape.
Past the point where there is any recognition of diamonds.
The son of the diamond merchant walks bare footed,
cutting his feet on his father's rocks;
his father takes him by the hand,
a pocket full of windows.
Dancing down the rough road,
there are eyes in his ankles and wrists. He focuses his eye
on a spot in the distance,
perhaps a sun in the mare's head nebula;
he turns on all his body,
and his body becomes a pocket of eyes.

The son of the diamond merchant looks for diamonds in the dark;
he found a diamond as big as his shoe
and requested to be buried with his boots on.
His father gave him a diamond as big as his eye
and requested the old eye be buried,
as his diamonds came out of the earth,
the mine itself being a pocket of eyes.
And then he told the stories of diamonds:
        it was said that in 1880
        a perfect crystal ball 10 inches in diameter
        was found in a pure vein of coal.

Count Rothschild
who owned the mine
gave the crystal to his eldest niece
who disappeared without a word
leaving her husband, Count X, and three children.
One day 20 years later,
the abandoned husband
received a distraught visit from
a dark-haired man with a beard who said that
20 years ago he married a woman with a crystal ball
whom he later found out to be Count X's wife;
she now had disappeared without a word to him, her husband,
or their two children.
Had Count X heard from her at all?
He brought to Count X her 6 carat diamond ring
as proof that she was the same woman.

As final proof that a certain child born in Tibet was to be
the new Dalai Lama,
his parents produced a small piece of crystal
that had been lodged under the child's tongue
at birth.

The diamond merchant himself was never sure that there was
anything more beautiful than a diamond,
or one of its substitutes.
He looked for diamonds everywhere.
In everything.
He always knew the prices.
And it was the price which determined my life.
Talk was not cheap either.

Your legacy of diamonds falls out of your teeth when you talk;
they are embedded in your throat rasping the sensitive membranes
when you try to speak.

The diamond
being the hardest stone
is used for cutting others.

The diamond cutter starts out with a piece of rock
as large as a large man's fist.
The diamond cutter spends hours analysing the veins of the mineral,
knows finally about every axis of the stone.
One blow,
one cut,
is the only necessity to make the stone fall away
revealing the perfect face of the gem.
That same
one cut
could shatter the rock,
could break it perhaps $50,000 worth
into chips scarcely as valuable as the hairs that fall out of your
head,
or the bones from a dead
animal's body.
The merchant makes sure
he employs a diamond cutter with enough skill
to recognize gems
from another solar system.

He must touch them in his sleep,
perhaps walk with the diamonds in his armpits or
under his tongue, in his mouth.
He may put the diamonds along with the golf balls and stars
into his pipe,
smoke them,
let them remember their pressurized origins.
He may smoke universes in his pipe and not know it.

If you know my name,
you know Diane comes across diamond in the word book,
crossing my life,
wealth comes out of the teeth and tongue of my mouth,
leaving me incomplete;
I sell myself
for high prices (as do we all)
my weight on a balancing scale traded for diamonds . . .

There is one man who knows me better than all others.
The merchant,
weighing off my fingers and toes
my brain as heavy as a grandfather clock,
my eyes sagging under their load of accusations,
every word hanging like the sack of cement on a murdered body
at the bottom of the river.

His diamond cutter knows my axis,
knows where to strike me for a clean break.

All life is barter and trade; exchange of valuable things.
Even you, who love me now,
love me for my valuables,
the diamonds you can pick out of my brain.
They were traded by the merchant
for a length of blood vein
or an ounce of dust from my lips or ears.
It is no surprise that the diamond merchant
in his black suit
is someone we all
know.

A LONG POEM FOR ELEANOR WHO
COLLECTS THE BLOOD OF POETS

This blood is very red & thick
having the political energy to keep warm
at night.
> My feet get very cold
> and I often wonder if there is
> something wrong with them,
> but I am told, it's a circulation problem.
> Blood again.
> The subject is too hot or too cold,
> all because of blood.

This blood is thick & it was very hard to get
out of the finger.
> My fingers have always had a very
> special significance to me;
> perhaps that is why I have been fascinated by
> & suspicious of rings
> for so long.

The only real subject of conversation these days
is justice. David says I have a very
wicked sense of justice. That is
true.
But I don't believe in physical sufferings.
I believe everyone should have to have emotional sufferings.
Those, we can all survive.
No one should ever have to shed blood
unless he wants to.
The blood of a poet is given
because the poet wants to see what
he's made of.
> Blood is manufactured in the bones.
> It would be somewhat harder to do,
> but mightn't you also start the bones
> of the poets

collection?
Question is
what constitutes the blood & bone
of a poet?
Or is he just like any other man?

Your collections
give me the feeling
that this country would be better off
if poets had nothing
to do
with government.
Poets giving their blood
so easily
give me the impression
that a poet is
always ready
to give his life
                his blood and bone
for what he believes.
Belief makes us choose between gladiolas
& carnations at best,
but it usually makes us hurt others.
Always because they've hurt us.
Or we're afraid they will someday hurt us.

Poets are too worried about hurting.
Too afraid of hurt.
Too willing to be hurt.
A man like that
couldn't make a good president.

The greatest disillusionment about poets
is that they don't practice what they preach.

Here is a lovely lady
stroking the ass of
what I must assume is another lovely lady
with a flower, a foxglove, perhaps
            or some 16th century version of
            a freesia, deadly nightshade another possibility . . .
Have you ever noticed the names of butterflies?
Some are quite beautiful,
like the dusky mourning moth,
or the timbered dusky moth,
or even the sky shattered steel mouthed moth. A wing,
a page,
the writing in somebody's book,
of poems?

I am honored to have my blood in your collection,
dusky wing,
lady of the Renaissance rose.

The blood that slips through our fingers every day
could be used to write a book
where everything is beautiful.
All parts of us grow. Not all our parts are living,
such as the teeth,
those hard nuts & bolts that keep us together.
Anything that is living
bleeds.

You are right to collect relics.
I have woven the butterfly wing into my skin,
have attached flowers to the bones in my ear,
have given all objects names
like stars.
Have timbered my roof
with blood relics.

ESOTERIC FABLES

A SHORT FABLE OF ENDURANCE AND PITY

*For a man who finds his present identity
unendurable.*

Once there was a buffalo who liked to eat mushrooms. However, he lived on the dry plains where mushrooms did not grow. At best, he could find buffalo grass, buttercups, and chicory. In fact, this buffalo had never even eaten mushrooms, but he had read about them in the Encyclopedia Britannica and knew that they were just what he had always wanted. One day, as he was wandering farther and farther away from his home, looking for mushrooms, he saw something in the grass which looked to him like a mushroom. But when he nudged it with his nose, it moved. Every time he touched it, it moved. Still, it looked like nothing more than a stone, or perhaps a puffball (though the buffalo did not really know what a puffball looked like). When the buffalo tried to grab it in his teeth, it moved again. Finally, after following the round-white-thing-which-moved for almost a mile with his nose, he said, "Are you a mushroom or not?"

The round-white-thing-which-moved said, "Yes, I am a mushroom. Or at least I think I am, though I have never seen a mushroom except in the Encyclopedia Britannica. However, I think I look just like the picture of a puffball, and I am very happy at last to know what I am."

"I am going to eat you if you are a mushroom," said the buffalo. "Because all of my life, I have wanted to eat mushrooms. I know that they are what I will like. How fortunate that at last I have found one. You are sure that you are a mushroom, aren't you?"

Now the round-white-thing-which-moved began to think it might not be so smart to continue to call himself a mushroom, if the buffalo wanted to eat mushrooms. Therefore, he replied, "I could be a stone. Stones are inedible."

The buffalo, who was disappointed, hung his head. He almost

cried, but decided that since never in his lifetime had he seen a mushroom, it was not so terrible if the present moment did not hold a mushroom. How could you miss something which you had never experienced? But there was no doubt that he was very sad indeed.

The round-white-thing-which-moved saw a tear in the buffalo's eye and that he was fighting hard to keep from crying. He himself knew disappointment, and even more truly, he knew the fascination of mushrooms, of the hours of reading the encyclopedia, of finding pictures, of learning varieties, and to him, the excitement of at last identifying himself, knowing that he belonged to a world which could describe and understand him. And he thought to himself, "But if I am a mushroom, why am I pretending to be a stone? If I am truly a mushroom, perhaps the most exciting and real thing which could happen to me is to be eaten."

Pretending that he had not seen the buffalo's one concealed tear, the round-white-thing-which-moved, said shyly, "I could be a stone, but I am really a mushroom. A puffball."

Then he stood still in the grass. Awaiting fate.

The buffalo bent his head to the ground and with his big teeth picked up the round-white-thing-which-had-moved, opened his mouth wide, thrust the round-white-thing-which-had-moved between his jaws, and began to chew. But the moment he bit down on the round-white-thing-which-was-now-holding-still, he broke several of his teeth, for the object was hard and smooth, and not soft as a mushroom should have been. He spit the round-white-thing-which-had-moved out on the ground, covered with blood, no longer looking like a puffball in the grass. To this day, the buffalo has not tasted a mushroom, for he disdains them, and has written an appendix to the encyclopedia article on how unfit for consumption the puffball is. While the round-white-thing-which-moved, now moves slowly and sadly across the prairie, knowing it is not a mushroom, not knowing what it is. It has most recently taken to calling itself, ironically, a rolling stone, since one day a passing car on the highway, filled with beautifully mustached young men looking out over the plains, was the source of a voice, calling out over the prairie, "Look. That must be a rolling stone," but the round-white-thing-which-moved found it hard to take such a pronouncement seriously. Nowhere in the Encyclopedia Britannica could it find an entry for "rolling stone."

How could that ever be a proper identity?

THE OWL AND THE SNAKE

Once there was an unhappy owl. He lived longing for a different shape. He did not like the night. The day was his favorite time, but the sun was hard on his eyes. He wanted to be sleek and long and slither along the cool ground during the day. He, in fact, fell in love with a snake. Her name was Snake In The Green Grass and she was beautiful, slender and graceful. She thought he was funny to look at and knew she ought to be afraid of him, because owls eat snakes.

However, he was so foolishly and helplessly in love with her. He waited every morning for her to slink out of her hole so that he could present her with some newly killed creature for breakfast. She did not like to tell him that she only ate once a week and he, in fact, simply thought that she was rejecting him by refusing each new mouse, or mole, or gerbil.

This owl lived for years in love with his little snake. They both remained unmarried. While she did not exactly find the owl attractive, she found that more and more she did not find other snakes attractive. She found herself wishing sometimes that they had fluffy feathers, or rounder eyes. She felt crippled without wings or feet. And the owl spent more and more time on the ground, wishing he could move smoothly, that he could slink along with speed and in silence, that he did not have to soar into the air in order to feel his body respond with elegance or grace.

This story is a sad one. Nothing happens in it because when you want something extravagant and out of reach, nothing can happen. Time will pass. You will develop strange ways. The owls will reject you and so will the snakes. You will never have what you want. You will not change the world. You will be an unhappy owl. Or a spinster snake.

128

THE CAT WITH THE BROKEN TAIL

Usually in fables, there are animals behaving like people. In this one, I have reversed that order and created people acting like animals. Except for the protagonist, of course.

Once there was a spotted pussycat with a long white tail. She lived with people but did not like to be unduly fondled. She found that people indulged in a lot of corny shit, like fussing and petting her. She was aloof. One day there were guests in the house and she was sitting under a rocker. The guest, who was a substantial lady studying karate, put her booted foot down and squashed the cat's tail. Oh, did that cat run, leap, screech, and yowl. Her fine upright white tail was undeniably broken. It hung like a kite caught in a tree. She was a cat with a broken tail. She went off to hide under the woodpile.

The guest felt remorseful, smitten with guilt, though she felt a bit self-righteous about not having any way to know there would be a cat under her chair. What could she do if, as she sat there, she put her foot down and found a cat underneath it?

The cat stayed under the woodpile for 5 days, during which the full moon changed to waning; during which a neighboring couple decided to get a divorce as they could not agree on whether the room they slept in should be dark or light in the morning; during which a whole crop of mushrooms came and went; during which the lady guest got her brown belt and telephoned to find out if the cat was O.K., and to offer a session of acupuncture to cure it when she heard the cat was missing.

But the owners of the cat knew it was under the woodpile and were so ashamed of this cowardly behavior they hung up quickly on the lady who broke the cat's tail.

Into this story comes an astronomer and a racing car driver,

129

both cat haters and, in fact, misogynists of the first order. They thought women were like stars or cars—to be gazed at or to be driven. They had no sympathy or love. They simply lived their own fascinating lives and did not care about anything else. The reason they come into this story is that both of them were friends of the family and happened to visit a week after the cat's tail had been broken, the racing car driver on his way to Indiana and the astronomer on his way to California.

When the racing car driver and the astronomer met each other, they hated each other almost as much as they individually hated cats and women. It was silly, they thought, for the whole family to be upset because a cat had broken its tail and was hiding under the woodpile, but though they both believed this, they hated each other so much that they would not admit that they agreed. While the racing driver was out tuning his engine, the astronomer surreptitiously went into the house and offered to lure the cat out from under the woodpile. But he did not know anything about cats, so he asked his hosts what he should do. Just then the lady brown belt who had broken the cat's tail arrived and bumped her car into the racing driver's car. He was so mad he hit her with a large wrench, and she hit him with a karate chop which sent him flying over to the woodpile, and when he thumped against it, the startled cat with the broken tail ran out and in its hysteria ran across the path of the lady brown belt who once again accidentally crushed the cat's tail. Now the poor cat's tail was broken in two places. The astronomer ran out of the house with his camera, photographed the lady brown belt who was inspecting her bruised arm from the wrench-strike, the cat with its tail broken in two places, and the racing car driver shakily picking himself up off the ground next to the woodpile; also the two cars which were slightly bashed together, and everything else which might help his photographs qualify for *National Geographic*. Then he set off for California with his film.

Ah ha. Now do you know what happened? The racing car driver picked up the cat and put a splint on its tail. The lady karate fighter went off to study aikidu, the art of disappearing which allows the grace of invisibility, as she was beginning to think that her feet and her body were always in the wrong places and going to

130

get her into serious trouble. The cat apologized for being so cowardly as to have stayed under the woodpile for a week, and the racing car driver went off to win some races.

CODA. Just because everyone lived happily ever after doesn't mean anything at all in this story. The reason that the cat is the protagonist of the story is that it was a victim and always had a funny looking tail afterwards. My favorite stories are inevitable and awful ones about how none of us ever changes his identity or really has anything too surprising happen to him. And most of us, in other people's eyes, live happily ever after. The astronomer hating cats and women and photographing them; the racing car driver hating cats and women and winding up helping them; the cat having the misfortune to be stepped on twice; no one really very much involved with anyone else's number.

Their fantasy lives are another matter. Only there can you find any excitement or surprise. Locked in your head is the only time you are not locked in your body.

THE FROG WHO WAS BORN WITH A WART ON
HIS NOSE

There was a frog who was born with a wart on his nose. He was handsome and self-assured, but the wart bothered him anyway. He wanted to have it removed, but the doctors told him he might lose his life if the wart were removed. This caused him to stay awake many nights wondering which was worse—to risk dying in order to have the wart removed or to live with the constant humiliation of that not-quite-perfect face, disfigured only by the wart—and with the worry that the wart would get larger or that it would multiply and that soon he might have several disfiguring warts. One night, as he lay worrying about his difficult situation, he saw a pelican asleep nearby. With its long beak folded under its wing, and its slender neck, it looked like a swan drifting in the water. The frog thought that the pelican was quite beautiful, and he was envious. Sure that this bird had never had to worry about anything like a wart on the nose, it suddenly occurred to him, as he sat thinking about the pelican, that probably very few of the beautiful creatures of the world ever had to worry about warts; that nature had been cruel to him, as it seldom was to other creatures.

He began to cry. At first softly, then louder and louder; his crying was filled with anguish and agony at his own terrible dilemma. The pelican awoke with the voice of the frog, weeping. He raised his long beak and quite suddenly looked like a different bird. Quite suddenly his appearance was different. Gawky, unclassical in every way. He started to say something in anger at being disturbed from his sleep, but the frog had been so astonished at the transformation of the sleeping pelican from an elegant creature to a gawky one, that he had not only stopped crying but also had almost forgot his own troubles. Since the pelican saw no reason to say anything now that the frog was quiet, he tucked his beak back under his wing and went to sleep. In the process, of course, being transformed into a lovely swan again . . .

The frog thought about this for a long time. About the facts of his own life, about the way he saw himself, about the very nature

132

of beauty itself. His thoughts were not comfortable ones, and it is to his credit that he thought them at all. But a vision of reality can come to anyone, even an otherwise handsome and narcissistic frog with a wart on his nose. I will let you, the reader, decide the outcome of the story, since vision is a personal experience, and none of us ever understands either what the other man sees in a moment of truth, or what he does with the perception after he sees that truth. A frog who thinks of his beauty seems ridiculous to those of us who are not frogs. At some moment we must all abandon everything, except perhaps comparison. The moment of truth when a swan is transformed into a pelican; when a frog considers the nature of beauty.

THE FABLE OF THE FRAGILE BUTTERFLY

Once upon a time there was a man who spent most of his time dreaming that he was a butterfly. His real profession was that of a garbage collector, and though he was paid well by the city government for which he worked, he could not bear to think too much of the fact that he earned his living as a collector of garbage. Consequently, he often dreamed that he was a butterfly. His wings were as long and blue as the neck of a peacock. His body was a cylinder of dusty yellow gold which, when the sun shone on it, winked and shone like the baton of a drum majorette twirling in the air. His antennae quivered like a dart which has just struck a hard board. He was fragile and fine. He knew his life was short. That he was like a sapphire glowing amidst great chunks of white bony fluted coral. In his dreams he flew farther than butterflies ever go, across oceans, sitting on the foamy crests of waves, flying across the desert, resting on the waxy blossoms of yucca plants, flying through back yards, in and out of pear trees and holly bushes, even occasionally through the city where his iridescent blue wings flashed like tropical beetles against the grey concrete. He was quiet and gentle, heaving garbage cans into the big grinding trucks which crushed tin cans, old food, papers and mateless shoes to a pulp. His fellow workers called him "the philosopher" because he always seemed lost in his own thoughts, smiling often but never really exchanging banter and jokes with the other workers.

One day however, while he was dreaming that he was a butterfly in the midst of a long journey through a mountainous land, he noticed as he peered down into the stream of garbage his man-body was pouring into the refuse truck, that something gold gleamed and shone, like a stream of honey-colored liquid just beyond his dark stained gloves. He looked down into the garbage and for a moment thought he saw an eye staring up at him. No, I'm dreaming, he thought. There is nothing here but pure garbage. I do not love my job, but I know that it is useful to people, that someone must process their garbage and that my real life in my head, my butterfly life, is enough pleasure for anyone. I will not delude myself into believing that there is something living and beautiful with an amber body and a cat's eye in this garbage.

So he continued to unload cans of filth and discarded objects, old food and crumbled plaster into the garbage truck each day. His iridescent blue body flew and shimmered over new landscapes, longer and longer journies which allowed him to meditate on distance, time, space, beauty and truth, all while he was quietly and gently disposing of the garbage city dwellers accumulate, serving the purposes of a clean world, aware that he was useful, even smiling occasionally when someone asked him in a bar after work what his job was. "I am a garbage collector," he would say.

One day as he worked, a large Monarch butterfly, orange and black and luminous as a stained glass window, landed on the lip of the garbage truck. As it did so, he thought once again that he saw gold, like liquid, pouring into his truck and that the eye of a tiger gleamed out at him. He blinked and peered down into the garbage but saw nothing remarkable, and the Monarch fluttered up and on its way.

Now to be true to the principle of my fable something should happen which would inevitably illuminate our vision of this man who believes he is a gorgeous butterfly but who really serves mankind as a garbage collector, zen-like confer the meaning of opposites, or perhaps existentially demonstrate that literal metaphors are the only metaphysic. However, what you must know first is that this man is a magician. Under the spell of another magician. I will not say a wicked one, for that is to imply that the mere exercise of power is wicked and to forget that at all times everyone has some other person in his power, tho often he is unaware of it. And of course as wise readers, you will have guessed that the visiting Monarch butterfly is, in fact, the beautiful sister of the garbage collector who is indeed a butterfly, blue as the neck of a peacock, and that the stream of gold liquid followed by the glimpse of an eye like a cat or tiger is the magician who has the garbage collector in his spell.

At this moment, there is another interruption in the train of

135

thought which the garbage collector has been pursuing: a passionate red-headed student with curly hair comes out on the sidewalk with a plastic bag full of garbage and when the garbage man takes it, the student heaps abuse on him for some reason, old angers pouring out on the collector of garbage who dreams he is a butterfly, who is really a magician enchanted by another magician. Many of us at times have to accept the angers heaped upon us by others who do not know us literally, who do not understand our fantasies or dream-life, who in fact are angry with themselves for inhabiting the wrong bodies, for not being beautiful enough . . . But transformations and concatenations are our own creations, consequently the Monarch butterfly, who is the sister of the garbage collector, flies around the head of the angry student and lands in his fiery hair. The butterfly is combusted instantly into flames, for the student's hair is really fire, so long has he been angry. When the garbage collector sees this, he cannot resist. He becomes himself, the blue butterfly, and flies away to a cool ocean, green covered with white spray, hurt by the reality and injustice of coincidence. While the enchanting magician who is amber melted into the garbage of city dwellers (who often do not recognize beauty when they see it untransformed) turns himself into a gigantic orange tom cat with blazing eyes who jumps out of the garbage truck and savagely claws the angry student, leaving scratches across his face; and of course there are the charred remains of a Monarch butterfly in the student's hair.

True to life, this story has many endings, some that occur immediately and others which require many years for fulfillment. Let me list some of them:

1. The world becomes dirtier with the loss of the collector who is really a blue butterfly, for few workers are so conscientious and uncomplaining about taking care of the garbage of others as he was.

2. The great magician war begins and plagues the earth for decades.

3. The meaning of amber and butterflies is changed.

136

4. The angry student becomes an angry man, unaware of his own power and thus a dangerous man to know. He eventually becomes president or king and tries to end the magician wars by setting the world on fire. His hair burns him when he sleeps at night.

5. Swiftly, the life of the Monarch sister has come to an end, and she is never heard of again. She did not leave any poetry behind to be read by posterity and she did not found a large corporation to carry on her name. Children do not believe in their parents, so it is irrelevant if she had any. They would not remember her as she was, anyway. Death is a matter of fact, a reminder to us all.

6. I, the speaker in this fable, will pretend to be the Sphinx and ask you this riddle: I am not a man dreaming that I am a butterfly, and I am not a butterfly dreaming that I am a man. Who am I?

7. Who are you?

Printed October 1973 in Santa Barbara for the Black Sparrow Press by Noel Young. Design by Barbara Martin. This edition is published in paper wrappers; there are 300 hardcover copies numbered & signed by the poet; & 50 copies handbound in boards by Earle Gray signed & with an original holograph poem by the poet.

PHOTO: THOMAS VICTOR

Diane Wakoski was born in California in 1937. The poems in her published books give all the important information about her life.